Alison Hodge

coast

featuring the work of

BOB BERRY

with an introduction by
Frank Ruhrmund

For the Hungarian-born French photographer Brassaï, famed for his photographs documenting Parisian night-life in the 1930s, there was only one criterion for a good photograph – 'That it be unforgettable'.

If Brassaï could be here now, could turn these pages, could walk, as it were, around the 'coast' in company with Yorkshire-born Cornish photographer Bob Berry, then he would be certain to agree that these photographs are not only unforgettable but also unusual, not to say, unique.

While capturing the essence of the coast of Cornwall, these photographs go beyond its boundaries, beyond the parish, beyond the particular, to speak of what Matthew Arnold called the 'poetic truth and poetic beauty' to be found in nature the world over. Indeed, to borrow further from that great nineteenth-century British poet and critic, it is no exaggeration to say that, like 'genuine poetry', so Bob Berry's photographs 'have been conceived and composed in the soul'. Not too surprising, perhaps, for a photographer who 'just loves taking pictures in one of the most beautiful, magical places on Earth'.

An entirely self-taught artist with the camera, Bob Berry's love of photography began early. As a small boy he would walk the streets, carrying his first camera, 'a little Kodak Instamatic', touting for business, 'asking people out walking their dogs if they minded having a photograph taken'.

It was not long before he left behind those innocent 'Instamatic' days and, via family holidays, graduated to taking photographs in Sweden using 'an old Exacta'. Anyone who has ever taken photographs will feel for him when he confesses that his first series of Swedish pictures was shot without a film in the camera!

One of Bob's finest moments came with the purchase of a Nikon FM: 'My first real camera, it took me nine months to pay for it before finally being allowed to carry it out of the shop and use it.' With his Nikon FM in hand, he was soon hot-footing it around the photographic studios and darkrooms of London, looking for work. Although he met with little success at first, he did meet with the talented black and white printer Gene Nocon – 'That was a real pleasure, I not only got a cup of tea, but also some great advice.'

For a time he trod the well-worn path of the beginner and learner, living rough while taking 'moody black and white pictures of back streets and people', and appreciating more and more the art and strengths of such photographers as Don McCullin, Eugene Smith, John Blakemore and Paul Wakefield.

Then, just over 20 years ago, travelling in the back of his parents' camper van, he came to the far west of Cornwall, to Coldharbour Barn, near St Ives. The family converted the barn to a dwelling, and for Bob 'it was a brilliant three or four years of knocking down, dropping huge bits of granite on my feet, wondering how on earth my first block wall was going to stay up, and of trips to the local tip to salvage anything of use. A time spent watching the sunset behind an old washing machine and a dumped Tesco trolley, it was a cracking time.'

As his building efforts neared their end, Bob was lucky enough to obtain a post as a lab technician with Lelant-based photographers, H. Tempest Ltd., which enabled him to save enough money, and with 'monumental help and encouragement from my Mum and Dad, two of my greatest friends', to start in business in his own right as a freelance photographer.

In 1987, he was invited by the directors of the Wolf at the Door Gallery in Penzance to hold an exhibition of his work there. 'I have to thank Lu and Anne, the two lovely ladies who ran the Wolf at the Door Gallery for their help and advice, for pushing me to get something on the gallery's walls. It was a time when photographs were rarely seen in an art gallery.' It was also a time that marked his start as an art photographer, and the time that I first came across Bob Berry's pictures and realized he was a photographer to be reckoned with.

Since that first solo show, despite the pressures of making a living as a commercial photographer, Bob has enjoyed a number of exhibitions of his landscape photographs. He has a passion for landscape and, in photographs that are as unforgettable as Brassaï could wish for, he allows us to see and feel the ebb and flow of tides; the elemental power that makes us feel tiny, insignificant, and not a little afraid. At the same time, Bob Berry's photographs are filled with the spirit of Cornwall, and with them he inspires and leaves his viewer, as Thomas Hardy was when coming home from Lyonesse – 'with magic in his eyes'.

Frank Ruhrmund

Cornwall. An ancient, granite
land. Almost an island, a long
way from the rest of Britain,
it has always been different,
and Penwith, its most westerly
point, is different again. Its
cliffs, its coastline, its crisp,
clear light...

Edwin Smith once wrote:
'The man who lives in his
eyes is continually confronted
with scenes and spectacles
that compel his attention or
admiration and demand an
adequate reaction. To pass on
without pause is impossible...
some tribute must be paid.
Photography is a convenient
and simple means of discharg-
ing this ever recurrent debt to
the visual world.' It is a meas-
ure of Bob's talent that his
pictures look easy, for they
are far from simple.

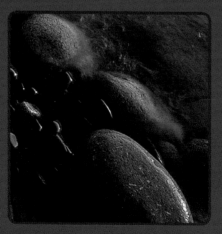

Crawl around the rocks, bend double to get under the 'belly' of some huge stone, wedge the Fuji 6 x 9 up against a rock, wonder why you didn't grow a third eye somewhere useful so you could catch a glimpse through the rangefinder, press shutter, reassuring clunk, take foot out of left ear, and move on.

11

It's been written and spoken about countless times by a thousand and one photographers, but it's all about that 'magic moment'. You point your camera, compose, shoot, and some time later the image you want, that special bit of the landscape, appears through a wash of liquid.

I guess it's the fact that you have to be out there to get it that makes photography so captivating. You're there for the experience and, hopefully, you bring back a reminder of that special moment, the time and place.

There's only one word to describe it — magic!

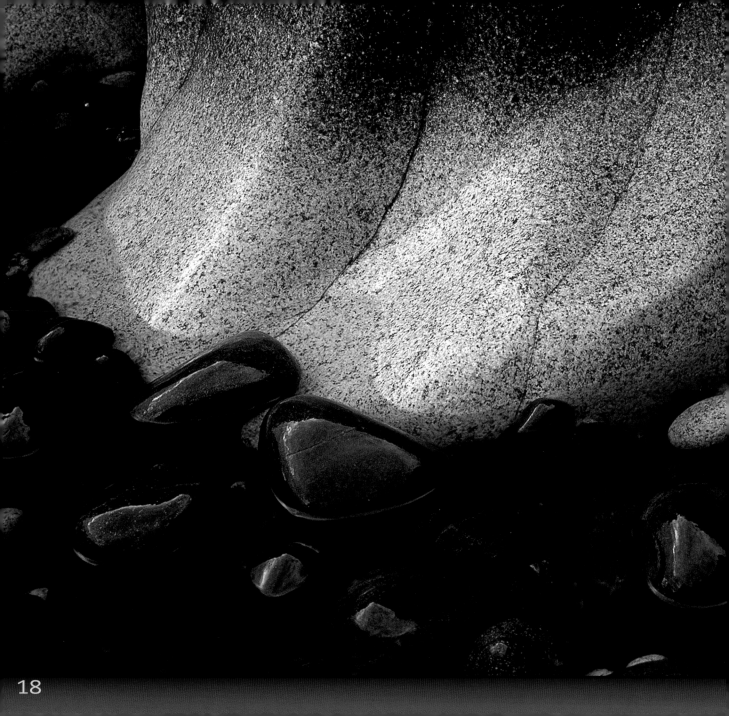

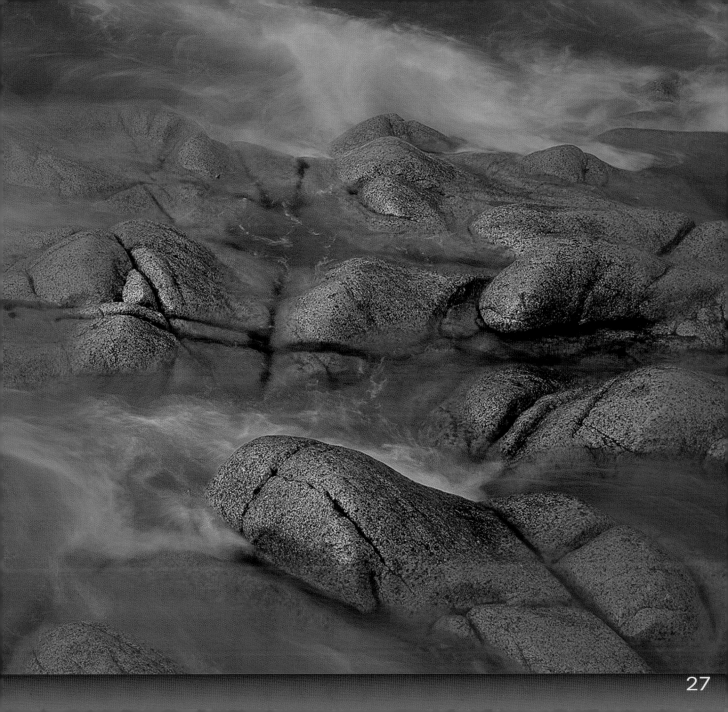

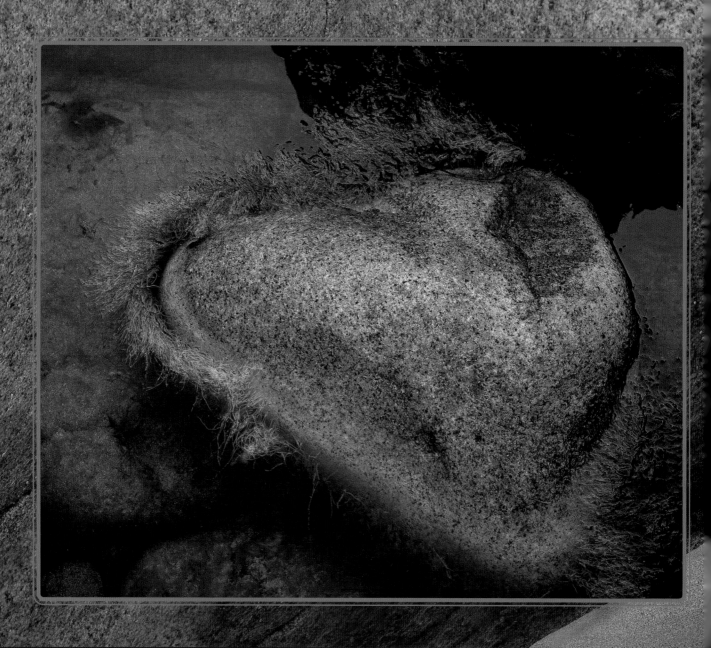

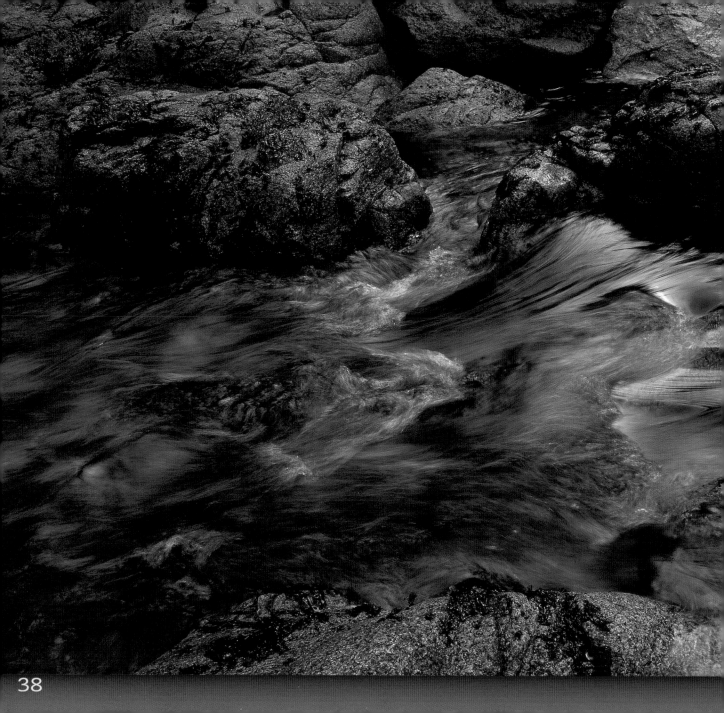

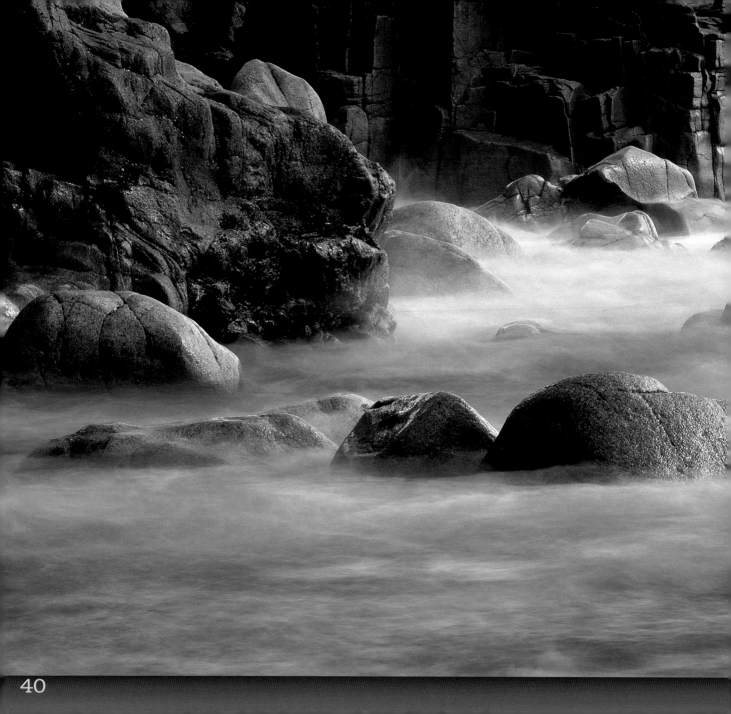

Since acquiring his first Instamatic at the age of nine, Bob Berry has used, owned and enjoyed a great variety of fine photographic equipment, and has exposed and processed film of all sizes – from 35mm (36 x 24) to 5 x 4 (inches). Today he is as much at home with a mahogany and leather bellows device as with the latest digital technology.

Cameras — What do I use? Anything and everything I can lay my hands on. Sometimes it's better to get out there and get a picture — some pictures — than to spend too much time wondering which is the best camera/ format to hump up the hill and down the other side. Chances are you take out the 5 x 4, and wish you could get that beautiful wave breaking over a rock that would have looked brilliant if you'd taken along the 80–200mm zoom for the 35mm... . Love experimenting with differ-ent formats — long and thin; square texture details; jump-ing about all over the place with 35mm. Something really great about setting up the 5 x 4 in a gale, behind a clump of rocks to stop the wind blowing the bellows like a mad

busker with an accordion ... slipping in the dark slide and watching your fingers freeze to the cable release as you wait patiently for that amazing wave to roll in and hit the rock you hoped you focused on correctly, dragging a few boulders with it ... a rumble like thunder ... spray flying up into the air as you release the shutter and let the light filter through the water during the one- or two-second exposure ... big panic as you watch salt-laden air crawling up the cliff towards the camera ... but hell, maybe you got the picture, and the UV filter will come clean with quick wipe over.

Humping heavy camera equipment can damage your back, and many a landscape photographer has welcomed the arrival of the compact Hasselblad X-Pan panoramic camera. Using two frames of 35mm film in panoramic mode, this rangefinder camera is an interesting mix of innovation and tradition.

The X-Pan ... what a corking bit of gear — almost small enough to fit in your pocket, produces really big-camera pictures!

Bob's 'darkroom'

But for portability and a huge range of lenses and accessories, the 35mm film format still rules.

There is something sweet about 35mm transparencies ... waiting for them to come back to see what you actually did take ... then spreading them out on a light-box, and just watching the light ooze through that patchwork of colours ... especially exciting with photographing the sea: that percentage of a long exposure when you just don't quite know how it's going to reproduce on film; how the light will kick back off the water; what patterns, shapes, distortions will appear ... no substitute for that feeling.

But sometimes you just can't wait to get your slides back. The recent, rapid growth of digital (filmless) photography has been driven, largely, by a desire for immediate accessibility. The growth has also been stimulated by the widespread expansion in the use of computers and the dramatic improvements in data transmission. (Today, a news photographer anywhere in the world, with a digital camera and a satellite telephone, can have an image on the picture editor's desk within minutes of taking it.) Early users of digital cameras traded a drop in picture quality for speed and convenience. Now, the output of good digital and film cameras is indistinguishable, and increasingly the image produced by either is treated as raw material in the creation of the final picture on a computer. Although many of his commercial clients still prefer to receive transparencies, Bob has enthusiastically embraced digital technology.

I love the commercial work too. The variety brings challenges and I get to meet and interact with loads of people, which I really like ... it balances the solitude of the landscape work.

Bob's workhorse 35mm film camera is a Nikon F5. He shoots digitally on a Fuji S1, which shares the Nikon lenses. For larger format work he uses a Sinar P2 with various rollfilm backs, and the X-Pan now covers most of the landscapes. Fujifilm Velvia and Kodak E100VS are his landscape films of choice.

www.bobberry.com

exhibitions (indicates solo exhibitions)

1999	The Strand Gallery, Newlyn, Penzance
	The Schoolhouse, Morvah, Penzance
1998	Amersfort, Holland
	Bakehouse Gallery, Penzance
1997–8	White Sands Lodge, Sennen
1997	Bakehouse Gallery, Penzance
1996	Edinburgh Exhibition – Peace, first prize
	Vospers, Penzance
	Bakehouse Gallery, Penzance
1995	Falmouth Marine School, Falmouth
	Bakehouse Gallery, Penzance
1994	Creftow, Helston
	Falmouth School of Art and Design
1993	Penzance and District Museum
1992	Rainyday Gallery, Penzance
	Wolf at the Door Gallery, Penzance
	Royal Cornwall Museum, Truro
	Falmouth School of Art and Design
	Creftow, Helston
1989	Street Gallery, Somerset
1988	Salon of Contemporary British Photography
	Wolf at the Door Gallery, Penzance
	Penlee House Museum, Penzance
	Visions and Journeys Gallery, St Just, Penzance
1987	Salon of Contemporary British Photography
	Wolf at the Door Gallery, Penzance
	Questra Gallery, Kingston-on-Thames
1986	Penzance Arts Centre

acknowledgements

Photographs are reproduced by kind permission of Jon Ailes: pp. 2–3; Christopher Laughton: pp. 1, 48–9. All other photographs are by Bob Berry.

First published in 2002 by **Alison Hodge**
Bosulval, Newmill, Penzance, Cornwall TR20 8XA.
info@alison-hodge.co.uk
www.alison-hodge.co.uk

Designed by **Christopher Laughton**.

© Bob Berry, 2002

The Author has asserted his right under the Copyright, Designs and Patents Act, 1988, to be identified as Author of this Work.

ISBN 0 906720 61 3

A catalogue record for this book is available from the British Library.

Originated by BDP –
Book Development and Production,
Penzance, Cornwall.

Printed and bound in Spain.